RASPBEI

COMPLETE MANUAL

A Step-by-Step Guide to the New Raspberry Pi 4 and Set Up Innovative Projects

Raphael Stone

Copyright © 2019 by Raphael Stone - All rights reserved.

All other copyrights & trademarks are the properties of their respective owners; Reproduction of any part of this book without the permission of the copyright owners is illegal-except with the inclusion of brief quotes in a review of the work

CONTENTS

Introduction..1

How to set up Raspberry Pi 4.......................................2

  What you need to set up Raspberry Pi 4.....................2

  Connect the keyboard, mouse, and monitor cables........7

Keyboard and mouse settings...9

  Set up Raspberry Pi OS: Raspbian............................12

Connecting to the internet..19

Setting up the sound...21

Installing software..22

Updating your Pi..27

Accessing your files..31

Using the terminal..36

Configuring your Pi...40

How to set up Windows 10 on the Raspberry Pi 4..........47

Qualitative review of Raspberry pi 4..............................59

Raspberry Pi Commands..78

  General Commands..80

  File and Directory Commands....................................81

  Networking and Internet Commands...........................83

System Information Commands.....................................84

Navigating the Raspberry Pi's Software.........................86

Getting Around...86

Using the Desktop Environment..............................87

Shutdown + Reboot from GUI................................92

Using the File Manager..94

Using the Command-Line Interface.........................95

Take a Screenshot!...98

Sudo, Root, and Permissions................................100

The Directory Tree...101

Getting Around and Creating Files.........................103

More Useful Command-line Stuff............................104

Programming basics using Python...............................109

What is Python?...109

Running python programs...111

Python Data types..113

What are iterators in Python?....................................121

Raspberry pi 4 Projects...131

Robot antenna...131

IoT Smart Garage Door Opener using Raspberry Pi.....146

Astronaut Reaction Time Game......................................158

Introduction

Congratulations on becoming a Raspberry Pi 4 explorer. We're sure you'll enjoy discovering a whole new world of computing and the chance to handcraft your own games, control your own robots and machines, and share your experiences with other Raspberry Pi fanatics.

Raspberry Pi 4 is now the newest and fastest Raspberry Pi you can get, which means way more functionality than ever before. With boosted specs over the Raspberry Pi 3 B+, like up to 4GB of RAM, this new single board computer is fit for some high-flying projects.

With the Pi 4 being faster, able to decode 4K video, benefiting from faster storage via USB 3.0, and faster network connections via true Gigabit Ethernet, the door is open to many new uses. It's also the first Pi that supports two screens at one -- up to dual 4K@30 displays -- a boon for creative who want more desktop space. This Complete Manual contains Raspberry Pi 4 projects, exercises and examples that will solidify your knowledge of programming. Let's get started!

How to set up Raspberry Pi 4

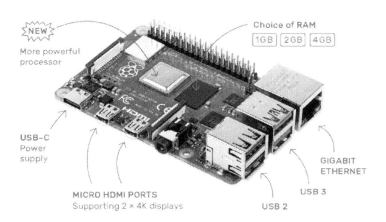

To get set up, simply format your microSD card, download NOOBS, and run the Raspbian installer. This guide will lead through each step. You'll find the Raspbian OS, including coding programs and office software, all available to use. After that, the world of digital making with Raspberry Pi awaits you.

What you need to set up Raspberry Pi 4

- **Raspberry Pi 4.** If you don't have many of the parts listed below you can buy a Raspberry Pi 4 desktop kit (which contains a Raspberry Pi 4, keyboard, mouse).

· Raspberry Pi 4 Kit

- **microSD card**. You'll need a microSD card with a capacity of 8GB or greater. Your Raspberry Pi uses it to store games, programs, and photo files and boots from your operating system, which runs from it. You'll also need a microSD card reader to connect the card to a PC, Mac, or Linux computer.

- **microSD card to SD card (or microSD card USB adaptor).** Many laptops have an SD card socket, but you'll need a microSD card to SD card adaptor to plug the small microSD card the Raspberry Pi uses to your computer. If your laptop does not have a SD card socket, you'll need a microSD card to USB Adaptor.

microSD card and microSD card to SD card adaptor

- **Computer.** You'll need a Windows, Linux PC (like the Raspberry Pi), or an Apple Mac computer to format the microSD card and download the initial setup software for your Raspberry Pi. It doesn't matter what operating system this computer runs, because it's just for copying the files across.

- **USB keyboard.** Like any computer, you need a means to enter web addresses, type commands, and otherwise control Raspberry Pi. You can use a Bluetooth keyboard, but the initial setup process is much easier with a wired keyboard. Raspberry Pi sells an official Keyboard and Hub.

- The Raspberry Pi Official Keyboard Hub

- **USB mouse**. A tethered mouse that physically attaches to your Raspberry Pi via a USB port is simplest and, unlike a Bluetooth version, is less likely to get lost just when you need it. Like the keyboard, we think it's best to perform the setup with a wired mouse. Raspberry Pi sells an Official Mouse.

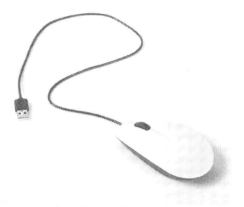

- Raspberry Pi mouse

- **Power supply**. Raspberry Pi uses the same type of USB power connection as your average smartphone. So you can recycle an old USB Type-C for Raspberry Pi 4 and a smartphone power supply (it should be a 15W power supply to provide effective power to the Raspberry Pi 4). Raspberry Pi also sells official power supplies, which provide a reliable source of power.

- Raspberry Pi Official Power Supply

- **micro-HDMI to HDMI cable**. Raspberry Pi 4 can power two HDMI displays, but requires a micro-HDMI to HDMI cable (if you want to reuse a regular HDMI cable you can also buy a micro-HDMI to HDMI adaptor).

· Micro HDMI to HDMI Cable

- **HDMI display**. A standard PC monitor is ideal, as the screen will be large enough to read comfortably. It needs to have an HDMI connection, as that's what's fitted on your Raspberry Pi 4 board.

Connect the keyboard, mouse, and monitor cables

Raspberry Pi 4 has plenty of connections, making it easy to set up. You'll interact with the Raspberry Pi using a keyboard and mouse

- **Connect the keyboard**. Connect a regular wired PC (or Mac) keyboard to one of the four larger USB A sockets on a Raspberry Pi 4. It doesn't matter which USB A socket you connect it to (although we think it's better to use the black connection, saving the faster blue one for other devices). It is possible to connect a Bluetooth keyboard, but it's much better to use a wired keyboard to start with.

- **Connect a mouse.** Connect a USB wired mouse to one of the other larger USB A sockets on Raspberry Pi. As with the keyboard, it is possible to use a Bluetooth wireless mouse, but setup is much easier with a wired connection. A regular wired mouse is connected to any of the USB A sockets. A wired keyboard is connected to another of the USB A sockets. If you have a Raspberry Pi 4, it's best to keep the faster (blue)

USB 3.0 sockets free for flash drives or other components.

- **Attach the micro-HDMI cable**. Next, connect Raspberry Pi to your display using a micro-HDMI cable. This can connect to either of the micro-HDMI sockets on the side of a Raspberry Pi 4, we prefer to attach it to HDMI 0, which is the one closest to the power socket. Connect the other end of the micro-HDMI cable to an HDMI monitor or television.

Keyboard and mouse settings

To set up your mouse and keyboard, select **Preferences** and then **Mouse and Keyboard Settings** from the menu.

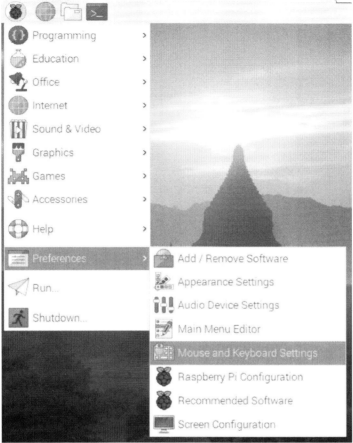

Mouse

You can change the mouse speed and double-click time here, and swap the buttons if you are left-handed.

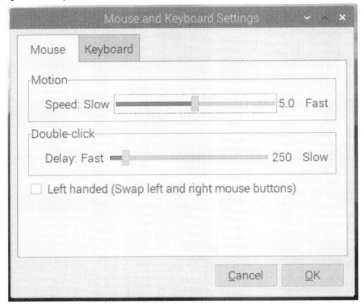

Keyboard

You can adjust the key repeat delay and interval values here.

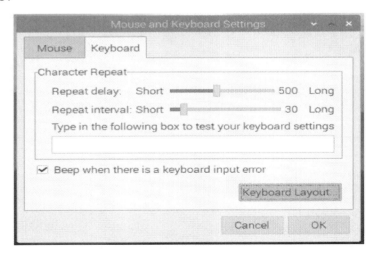

To change the keyboard layout, click on Keyboard Layout and select your layout from the list of countries.

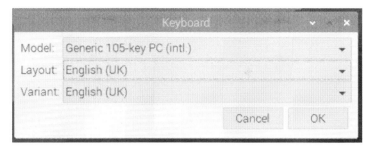

Set up Raspberry Pi OS: Raspbian

Now you've got all the pieces together, it's time to install an operating system on your Raspberry Pi, so you can start using it. Raspberry Pi uses a custom operating system called **Raspbian** (based upon a variant of Linux called 'Debian').

We're going to use a set of software called **NOOBS** (New Out Of Box Software) to install Raspbian OS on your microSD card and start your Raspberry Pi

Raspbian is the official OS for Raspberry Pi, and the easiest way to set up Raspbian on your Raspberry Pi is to use **NOOBS** (New Out Of Box Software).

If you bought a NOOBS pre-installed 16GB microSD card, you can skip Steps 1 to 3. Otherwise, you'll need to format a microSD card and copy the NOOBS software to it.

1. Download SD Card Formatter tool

Start by downloading SD Card Formatter tool from the SD Card Association website. Now attach the microSD card to your PC or Mac computer and launch SD Card Formatter (click **Yes** to allow Windows to run it). If the card isn't automatically recognised, remove and reattach it and click **Refresh**. The card should be selected automatically (or choose the right one from the list).

· SD Card Formatter

2. Format the microSD

Choose the **Quick Format** option and then click **Format** (if using a Mac, you'll need to enter your admin password at this point). When the card has completed the formatting process, it's ready for use in your Raspberry Pi. Leave the microSD card in your computer for now and simply note the location of your duly formatted SD card. Windows will often assign it a hard drive letter, such as E; on a Mac it will appear in the Devices part of a Finder window.

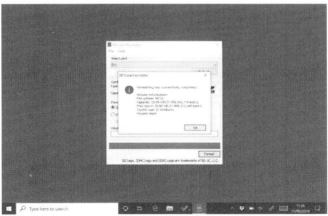

· Formatting a micro SD card with SD Card Formatter

3. Download NOOBS

Download the NOOBS software from Raspberry Pi. Choose Download Zip (or use the Torrent file if you're experienced with torrents and wish to save Raspberry Pi the bandwidth). NOOBS (New Out Of Box System) provides a choice of Raspberry Pi operating systems and installs them for you. Click 'Download zip' and save the file to your Downloads folder. When the zip file download is complete, double-click to launch and uncompress the folder. You'll need to copy all the files from the NOOBS folder to your SD card. Press CTRL+A (⌘+A on a Mac) to select all the files, and then drag all the files to the SD card folder. Once they've copied across, eject your SD card. Be careful to copy the files inside the NOOBS folder to the microSD card (not the NOOBS folder itself).

• Copy files from the NOOBS zip file to the micro SD card

4. Insert the microSD card to Raspberry Pi 4

Now it's time to physically set up your Raspberry Pi. Flip over Raspberry Pi 4 and locate the microSD card socket underneath. Carefully insert the microSD card. It will only fit in one way around, so if it's struggling to go in flip the microSD card over. Once it's inserted all the way in, it's time to start up your Raspberry Pi. Check that your PC monitor is plugged into the mains and that the HDMI cable is running to the corresponding HDMI port on your Raspberry Pi. Check that both the keyboard and mouse are connected to USB ports on Raspberry Pi 4.

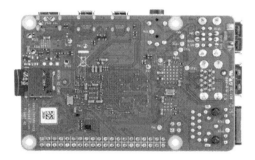

· Insert the micro SD card into the Raspberry Pi

5. Power up

Plug in your Raspberry Pi power supply and, after a few seconds, the screen should come on. When the NOOBS installer appears, you'll see a choice of operating systems. We're going to install Raspbian, the first and most popular one. Tick this option and click Install, then click Yes to confirm. For more OS options, instead click 'Wifi networks' and enter your wireless password; more OS choices will appear. Installation takes its time but will complete – eventually. After this, a message confirming the success installation appears. Your Raspberry Pi will prompt you to click OK, after which it will reboot and load the Raspbian OS.

- The NOOBS interface

6. Welcome to Raspberry Pi

When Raspbian loads for the first time, you will see this Welcome screen:

- Welcome to Raspberry Pi

Click Next, when prompted, then select your time zone and preferred language and create a login password. You're now ready to get online. Choose your WiFi network and type any required password. Once connected, click Next to allow Raspbian to check for any OS updates. When it's done so, it may ask to reboot so the updates can be applied.

Now you're ready to start using Raspberry Pi. Click the Raspberry Pi icon at the top-left of the screen to access items such as programming IDEs, a web browser, media player, image viewer, games, and accessories such as a calculator, file manager, and text editor. You're all set to start enjoying your very own Raspberry Pi.

Connecting to the internet

If you want to connect your Raspberry Pi to the internet, you can plug an Ethernet cable into it (if you have a Pi Zero, you'll need a USB-to-Ethernet adaptor as well).

If your model is a Pi 4, 3 or a Pi Zero W, you can also connect to a wireless network.

Connecting to a wireless network

Click on the wireless network icon in the top right-hand corner of the screen, and select your network from the drop-down menu.

Type in the password for your wireless network, then click OK.

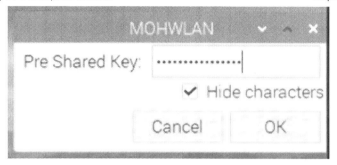

Once your Pi is connected to the internet, you will see a wireless LAN symbol instead of the red crosses.

Test your connection by clicking on the web browser icon and searching the web for raspberry pi.

Setting up the sound

Your Raspberry Pi can either send sound to the screen's built-in speakers through the HDMI connection (if your screen has speakers), or to the analog headphone jack.

Right-click on the speaker icon in the top right-hand corner to choose whether your Pi should use the HDMI or Analog connection for sound.

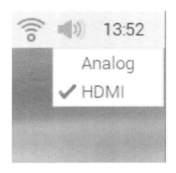

Click on the speaker icon to adjust the volume by moving the slider up or down.

Installing software

There are many, many software programs and applications you can download and install on the Raspberry Pi.

Note: your Pi has to be connected to the internet before you can install software. In the menu, click **Preferences** and then **Recommended Software**.

You can browse all the recommended software, or filter it by category.

To install a piece of software, click to mark the check box to its right.

Then click OK to install the selected software.

In addition to the Raspberry Pi's recommended software, there's a huge library of other available programs and applications. Click Preferences and then Add / Remove Software in the menu.

You can search for software, or browse by selecting a category from the menu on the left.

Let's try installing a drawing application called Pinta. Type 'pinta' into the search box and press Enter. Select Simple drawing/paint program in the list that appears.

Click OK to start the installation process.

When prompted, enter your password; if you haven't changed the password, it will be 'raspberry'.

Pinta will now be downloaded and installed.

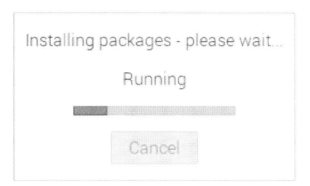

When the process is complete, open Pinta by selecting Graphics and then Pinta from the menu.

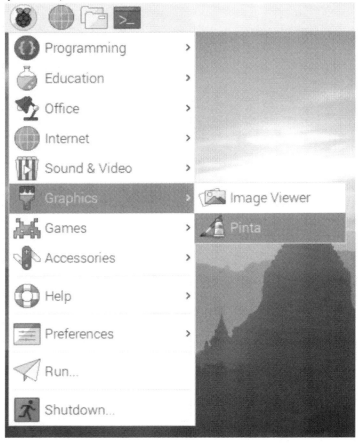

Updating your Pi

It's a good idea to regularly update the software on your Pi with the latest features and fixes. You can update your Pi using the Add / Remove Software application: open it by selecting it from the Preferences section of the menu.

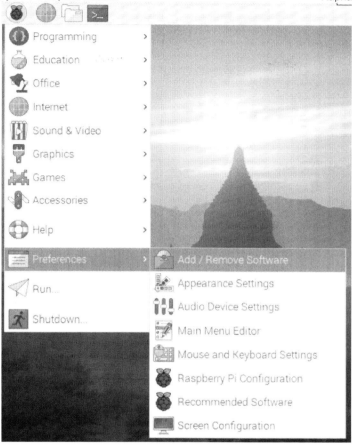

Before you check and install any updates, you should refresh the software package lists on your Pi. Click Options in the top left-hand corner, and select Refresh Package Lists.

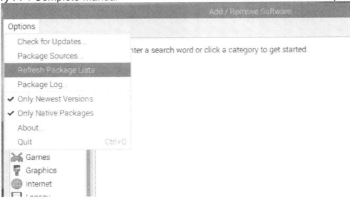

Your Pi will then update all lists of packages.

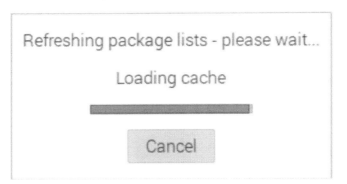

When this is done, click Options and select Check For Updates.

The Package Updater will open and automatically check whether updates are available. It will display anything it finds in a list.

Click Install Updates to install all the available updates. When prompted, enter your password; if you haven't changed the password, it will be 'raspberry'.

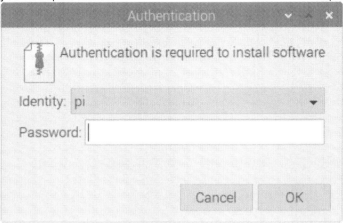

The updates will then be downloaded and installed. You can see the installation by checking the progress bar in the bottom left-hand corner.

Accessing your files

All the files on your Raspberry Pi, including the ones you create yourself, are stored on the SD Card. You can access your files using the File Manager application. Click Accessories and then File Manager in the menu, or select the File Manager icon on the menu bar.

When the file manager opens, you will be shown the pi directory — this is where you can store your files and create new subfolders.

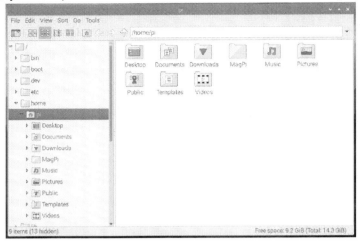

Double-click on the Documents icon to open the directory and view the files inside.

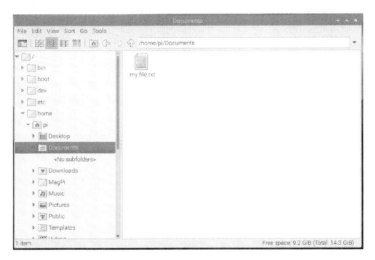

To open a file, double-click its name, or right-click it to open the file menu for more option.

You can use USB drives and sticks with your Raspberry Pi. This is a convenient way of backing up your files and copying them to other computers.

Insert a USB stick into your Raspberry Pi. A window will pop up, asking what action you want to perform.

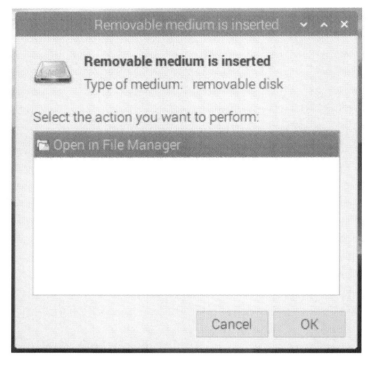

Click OK to Open in File Manager. The File Manager will open and show you the files on your USB stick.

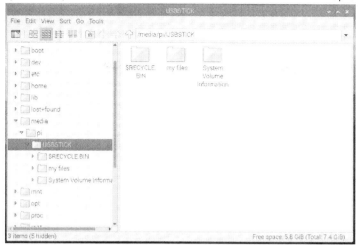

Using the terminal

The terminal is a really useful application: it allows you to navigate file directories and control your Pi using typed commands instead of clicking on menu options. It's often in many tutorials and project guides, including the ones on our website.

To open a terminal window, click on the Terminal icon at the top of the screen, or select Accessories and then Terminal in the menu.

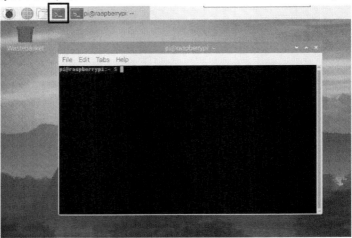

You can type commands into the terminal window and run them by pressing Enter on your keyboard. In the terminal window, type:

ls

Then press Enter on the keyboard. The command ls lists all the files and subdirectory in the current file directory. By default, the file directory that the terminal accesses when you open it is the one called pi.

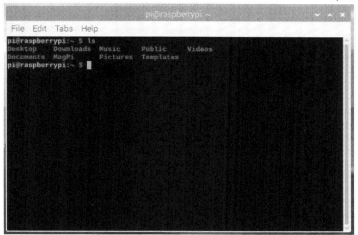

Now type in this command to change directory to the Desktop.

cd Desktop

You have to press the Enter key after every command. Use the command ls to list the files in the Desktop directory.

The terminal can do a lot more than list files — it's a very powerful way of interacting with your Raspberry Pi! As just one small example, try the command pinout:

pinout

This will show you a labelled diagram of the GPIO pins, and some other information about your Pi.

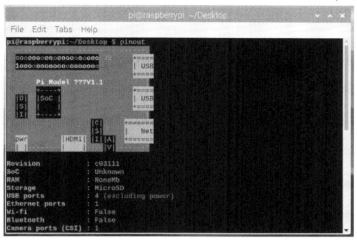

Close the terminal window by clicking on the x or using the command exit.

Configuring your Pi

You can control most of your Raspberry Pi's settings, such as the password, through the Raspberry Pi Configuration application found in Preferences on the menu.

System

In this tab you can change basic system settings of your Pi.

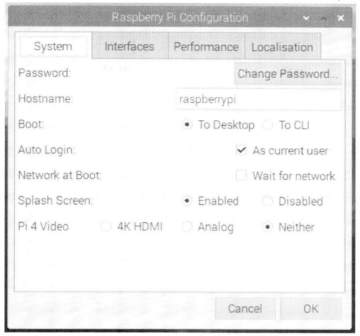

- **Password** — set the password of the pi user (it is a good idea to change the password from the factory default 'raspberry')
- **Boot** — select to show the Desktop or CLI (command line interface) when your Raspberry Pi starts
- **Auto Login** — enabling this option will make the Raspberry Pi automatically log in whenever it starts

- **Network at Boot** — selecting this option will cause your Raspberry Pi to wait until a network connection is available before starting
- **Splash Screen** — choose whether or not to show the splash (startup) screen when your Raspberry Pi boots

Interfaces

You can link devices and components to the Raspberry Pi using a lot of different types of connections. The Interfaces tab is where you turn these different connections on or off, so that the Pi recognizes that you've linked something to it via a particular type of connection.

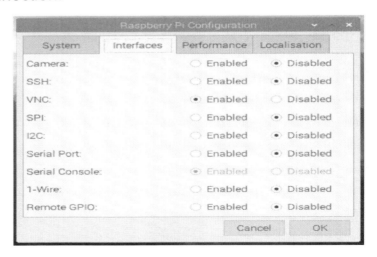

- **Camera** — enable the Raspberry Pi Camera Module
- **SSH** — allow remote access to your Raspberry Pi from another computer using SSH
- **VNC** — allow remote access to the Raspberry Pi Desktop from another computer using VNC
- **SPI** — enable the SPI GPIO pins
- **I2C** — enable the I2C GPIO pins
- **Serial** — enable the Serial (Rx, Tx) GPIO pins
- **1-Wire** — enable the 1-Wire GPIO pin
- **Remote GPIO** — allow access your Raspberry Pi's GPIO pins from another computer

Performance

If you need to do so for a particular project you want to work on, you can change the performance settings of your Pi in this tab.

Warning: changing your Pi's performance settings may result in it behaving erratically or not working.

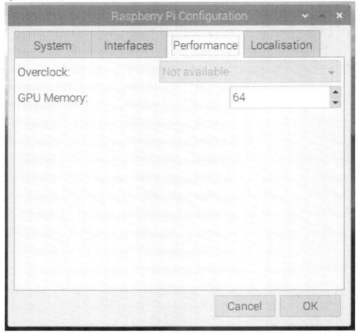

- **Overclock** — change the CPU speed and voltage to increase performance
- **GPU Memory** — change the allocation of memory given to the GPU

Localisation

This tab allows you to change your Raspberry Pi settings to be specific to a country or location.

- **Locale** — set the language, country, and character set used by your Raspberry Pi
- **Timezone** — set the time zone
- **Keyboard** — change your keyboard layout
- **WiFi Country** — set the WiFi country code

How to set up Windows 10 on the Raspberry Pi 4

Microsoft's ambition is for Windows 10 to run on every type of computing device, even the credit card-sized $35 Raspberry Pi board.

The Pi doesn't run the same version of Windows 10 as a laptop does, but a far simpler, stripped-back release called Windows 10 IoT Core.

This OS won't boot you into the traditional Windows desktop, but instead loads a bare bones menu from which you can set up the system, which can only run a single Universal Windows Platform (UWP) app with a GUI at a time.

The real purpose of Windows 10 IoT Core on the Pi is to run small applications, which are deployed to the board from a PC. These apps could do anything from taking readings from a temperature sensor, to acting as a simple web server.

But how do you get started? Here's a step-by-step guide to setting up Windows 10 IoT Core on the Raspberry Pi 2, 3 or 4, and then deploying a simple app, using a Windows 10 PC as the base machine.

Step 1. First you need to download NOOBS from the Raspberry Pi Foundation website. The NOOBs installer will make it easier to get Windows 10 IoT Core onto your Pi. Next get an SD card, which is 4GB or larger, and format it as FAT.

Format EFIESP (D:)   ×

Capacity:

Unknown capacity

File system

FAT (Default)

Allocation unit size

Default allocation size

Restore device defaults

Volume label

Format options

☑ Quick Format

Start   Close

Step 2. Extract the files from the downloaded NOOBs zip file. Copy the extracted files into the root directory of the card, making sure you are copying the files themselves, rather than a directory containing the files.

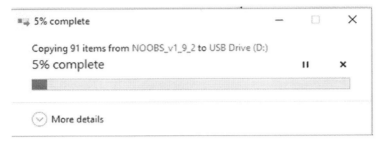

Step 3. Insert the SD card into the Raspberry Pi and boot the machine, ensuring the Pi is hooked up to a network.

You will see a drop-down list of operating systems, from which you should select Windows 10 IoT Core, as shown below. Confirm you want to overwrite the contents of the SD card - unless the card contains data you want to keep.

Choose from either the RTM, the latest official release of Windows 10 IoT Core, or the latest Windows 10 IoT Core Insider version (which requires you to have a Microsoft account set up for Insider access). Press OK and the machine will reboot into Windows 10 IoT Core once it has installed.

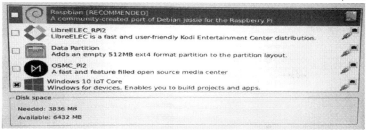

Step 4. Next you'll need to return to your main Windows machine and download and install Visual Studio, the IDE used to write code and deploy it to the Raspberry Pi.

The free edition of Visual Studio is known as Visual Studio Community 2015 and can be downloaded from here. Run the setup program and select the Custom option under Choose the type of installation. This will open the dialog box below, where you should tick the box marked Universal Windows App Development Tools, as shown. Click Next and then click Install.

The setup program will now download and install Visual Studio, be prepared to leave it for some time due to the large file size.

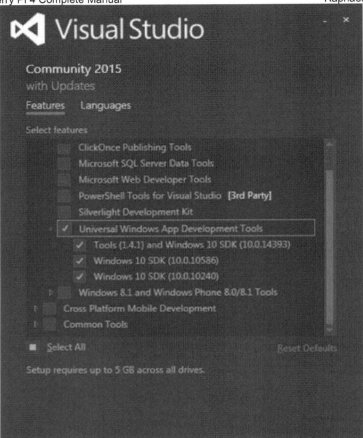

Step 5. Once the setup program has finished installing and updating you should have the correct version of Visual Studio. To check, open Visual Studio and select Help-> About Microsoft Visual Studio and check that the version is Visual Studio 14.0.25123.00 Update 3 or later. Also, in the list of Installed products in the window,

check that Visual Studio Tools for Universal Windows Apps is version 14.0.25527.01 or later.

Step 6. Now you need to enable developer mode on Windows 10. Go to Settings->Update & security. Select For developers in the lefthand list. As shown below, under Use developer features select Developer mode, and accept the disclaimer by clicking 'Yes'.

Step 7. For this guide, you'll need to install the latest Node.js Tools for UWP Apps. Before you do you need to make sure you have Git and Python installed on your machine.

Next you need to make sure that the location of Python and Git are stored in Windows' PATH environment variable. To do this, type System into the search box on the Taskbar. Left click on System Control Panel, then select Advanced system settings->Environment Variables. This should open the Environment Variables window, seen below. In the System variables box, double left click on Path. In the window Edit environment variable, click the button New to add the file location of Git and then do the same for Python, if they're not already included.

You can find the file location of both by typing either Git or Python into the search box on the Taskbar, and right clicking on the app and selecting Open file location. If this takes you to a Shortcut, then right click on the Shortcut to the app and inspect Properties and you'll find the location in the Start in field. Now you can install Node.js Tools for UWP Apps from here (if you're reading this sometime after publication check here for the latest release).

Step 8. Now start, or restart, Visual Studio 2015 and create a new project by going to File -> New Project. In the New Project window, click in the sidebar on Installed -> Templates -> JavaScript -> Node.js. Choose

the template for Basic Node.js Express 4 Application (Universal Windows), as shown below.

Step 9. The package manager npm will then install all of the software dependencies of the sample Node.js application that will be deployed to the Raspberry Pi. Wait until the dependencies have been downloaded, after which you should see the following directory structure in Visual Studio's Solution Explorer window.

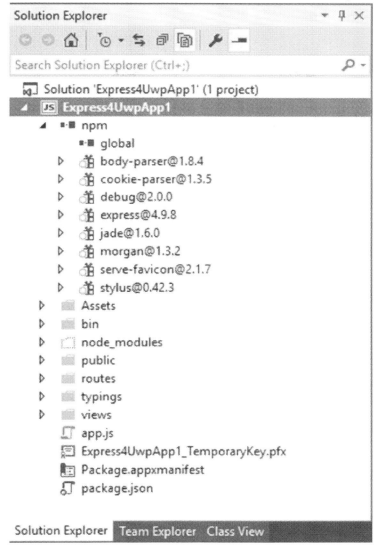

Step 10. Now you need the IP address of your Raspberry Pi. There are several ways of finding this, one way is to boot up Windows 10 IoT Core on the Pi.

The menu screen displays the IP address, as shown below.

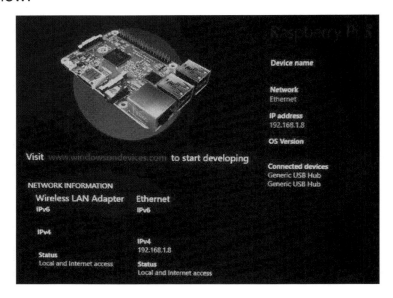

Step 11. Return to the sample app you created in Visual Studio and go to the Project-> Properties in the top menu. This should open a tab called Express4UWPApp1. In the field labelled Remote Machine, enter the IP address for the Raspberry Pi. At the top of the window is a dropdown menu labelled Platform, select ARM, as shown below.

Step 12. Press F5 to deploy the code to the Raspberry Pi. Be aware the deployment can take some time. When the app has been deployed to the Pi you should see the Ready message, as shown below, at the bottom of Visual Studio. The app should now be running and, if you're so inclined, ready to debug.

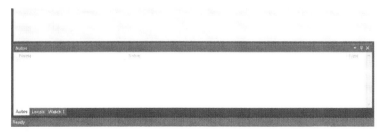

Step 13. Now to check the sample app is working. The code in this demo effectively sets up the Pi as a local web server, which can be accessed from your PC by opening a web browser, and typing http://[IP address of

the Pi]:3000. You should see a message saying 'Welcome to Express', as shown below.

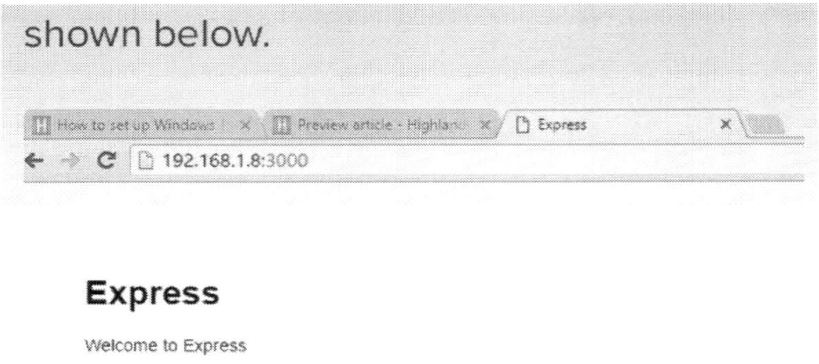

This is a very simple guide to installing Windows 10 IoT Core on the Pi and deploying a test app.

Qualitative review of Raspberry pi 4

WHAT IS THE RASPBERRY PI 4?

The Raspberry Pi 4 Model B is the latest version of the low-cost Raspberry Pi computer. The Pi isn't like your typical device; in its cheapest form it doesn't have a case, and is simply a credit-card sized electronic board -- of the type you might find inside a PC or laptop, but much smaller.

It costs as little as $35, although you might want to choose the $55 version with its 4GB of RAM for its better all-round performance.

WHAT IS THE RASPBERRY PI 4 CAPABLE OF?

The Raspberry Pi 4 can do a surprising amount. Amateur tech enthusiasts use Pi boards as media centers, file servers, retro games consoles, routers, and network-level ad-blockers, for starters. However that is just a taste of what's possible. There are hundreds of projects out there, where people have used the Pi to build tablets, laptops, phones, robots, smart mirrors, to take pictures on the edge of space, to run experiments on the International Space Station -- and that's without mentioning the more wacky creations -- teabag dunker anyone?

With the Pi 4 being faster, able to decode 4K video, benefiting from faster storage via USB 3.0, and faster network connections via true Gigabit Ethernet, the door is open to many new uses. It's also the first Pi that supports two screens at one -- up to dual 4K@30 displays -- a boon for creative who want more desktop space.

HOW DO I GET STARTED WITH THE RASPBERRY PI 4?

One thing to bear in mind is that in its cheapest form, the Pi is just a bare board. You'll also need a power supply, a monitor or TV, leads to connect to the monitor -- typically a micro HDMI cable -- and a mouse and keyboard.

Once you've hooked up all the cables, the easiest way for new users to get up and running on the Pi is to download the NOOBS (New Out-Of-Box Software) installer. After the download finishes, follow the instructions here and it will walk you through how to install an OS on the Pi. The installer allows you to install various operating systems, although a good choice for first time users is the official OS, which is called Raspbian.

The look and feel of Raspbian should be familiar to any recent desktop computer user. The OS, which is constantly being improved, has had several graphical overhauls, most recently to give its interface a minimalistic look, and includes an optimized web browser, an office suite, programming tools, educational games, and other software.

HOW IS THE RASPBERRY PI 4 DIFFERENT FROM ITS PREDECESSORS?

The quad-core Raspberry Pi 4 Model B is both faster and more capable than its predecessor, the Raspberry Pi 3 Model B+. For those interested in benchmarks, the Pi 4's CPU -- the board's main processor -- is offering two to three times the performance of the Pi 3's processor in some benchmarks.

Unlike its predecessor, the new board is capable of playing 4K video at 60 frames per second, boosting the Pi's media center credentials. That's not to say, however, that all video will play this smoothly, and supporting this hardware acceleration for H.265-encoded video is currently a work in progress across the Pi's various operating systems, so this is more a potential future feature than something available today.

The Pi 4 also supports wireless internet out of the box, with built-in Wi-Fi and Bluetooth.

The latest board can also boot directly from a USB-attached hard drive or pen drive, and, following a future firmware update, will support booting from a network-attached file system, using PXE. Using a network-attached drive is useful for remotely updating a Pi and for sharing an OS image between machines.

CAN I USE THE RASPBERRY PI 4 AS A DESKTOP PC?

The Pi can be run as a budget desktop, and with the release of the Pi 4 it's never worked better. The biggest benefit for everyday use -- office apps, web browsing, accessing online services -- is the additional memory.

With 4GB RAM, the Pi 4 no longer struggles with heavy web pages and apps, and is able to switch between full online services such as Google's G Suite and today's JavaScript laden sites without lagging. In many respects, it feels little different to a PC costing many times the price -- thanks to the improved specs and the lightweight yet capable Raspbian desktop.

CAN I WORK ON A RASPBERRY PI 4?

Yes, you can. It's obviously not going to be the same as a high-end laptop, as you're still talking about running a computer on a mobile-targeted processor, but as mentioned the performance is good enough that there's little to complain about.

With the gradual move from software to online services, the browser is increasingly the only application that a computer needs to run, and on that front the Pi 4 excels, thanks to the extra memory and the Raspberry Pi Foundation's work on optimizing Raspbian's default Chromium browser.

In fact, in the weeks after the Pi 4's release, the areas that are lacking on the Raspbian desktop tend to be related to video playback, although this is due to be addressed by a future software update, and work is continuing on improving 4K playback on media center operating systems such as LibreELEC.

However, the Pi works also well as a thin-client, as I found when I tested its capabilities when running it as a thin client for Windows 10, with performance being almost indistinguishable from running a modern Windows 10 PC, save for the very slow transfer of data to USB sticks. This was based on a Pi 3, so a Pi 4 with its true Gigabit Ethernet should work even better as a thin client.

CAN I BROWSE THE WEB USING THE RASPBERRY PI 4?

Yes, the latest version of the Raspberry Pi's official OS has the Chromium browser, the open-source browser that Chrome is based on. As mentioned, its performance on the 4GB Pi 4 is good, with little lag even on heavy sites, with the only wrinkle being screen tearing on YouTube video at launch, although this is due to be fixed with an update.

CAN I USE THE RASPBERRY PI 4 AS A MEDIA CENTER?

Yes, there are various options if you want to use the Pi 4 as a media center but the most popular choices are the Kodi-based OSes OSMC or LibreElec.

The Pi 4 has the added advantage of a faster and newer CPU and graphics processor, which the Raspberry Pi Foundation has said should be able to play local H.265-encoded video recorded at 3840 x

2160 resolution and 60 frames per second -- although support for this acceleration is still being implemented across the Pi's operating systems. Another advantage is built-in support for Wi-Fi, which makes it easier to stream content to the Pi, while native Bluetooth simplifies the hooking up peripherals.

CAN THE RASPBERRY PI 4 RUN PS1, N64, SNES, NES AND OTHER CLASSIC CONSOLE GAMES?

Yes, a wide range of vintage games will run on the Pi with the help of emulators like RetroPie, including some games from all of the systems listed above, although the more recent the system, the more likely it is that more demanding titles will struggle.

WHICH OPERATING SYSTEMS CAN I RUN ON THE PI?

The Pi can run a large range of systems, including the official Raspbian OS, Ubuntu Mate, Snappy Ubuntu Core, the Kodi-based media centers OSMC and LibreElec, the non-Linux based Risc OS (one for fans of 1990s Acorn computers). It can also run Windows 10 IoT Core, which is very different to the desktop version of Windows, as outlined below.

However, these are just the officially recommended operating systems, and a large array of other OSes also work on the Pi.

CAN THE RASPBERRY PI 4 RUN WINDOWS 10?

Yes, but it's nothing like the full desktop version of Windows 10 that most people are familiar with. Instead the Pi 3 runs Windows 10 IoT Core, a cutdown version of Windows 10 that doesn't boot into the graphical desktop and is designed to be controlled via a command line interface on a remote computer. It can only run a single fullscreen Universal Windows Platform app at a time, for example a kiosk app for a retail store, although other software can run in the background.

However, the Pi can act as a Windows 10 thin client, where Windows 10 is run on a server and streamed to the Pi and, with a powerful enough server, the experience can be virtually identical to running a Windows 10 machine. With the additional power of the Pi 4, and its dual-display support, the Pi's co-creator Eben Upton says he expects the Pi to make further inroads into the thin client market.

Upton says he feels the Pi 4 also likely has the power to run a full desktop version of Windows on Arm, but that any decision to port Windows to the Pi 4 rests with Microsoft.

CAN THE RASPBERRY PI 4 RUN WINDOWS 10 DESKTOP APPS?

The Pi 4 can run Windows desktop apps, although it requires an awful lot of effort to do so, and even then apps will only run poorly.

It used to be possible to do so using the ExaGear Desktop software, although this is no longer on sale. There are free alternatives, however, such as Pi386.

Whichever approach you use, performance will be sub-par, with the tools needed to run Windows apps on the Pi requiring so much processing power that you're basically restricted to running 20-year-old Windows apps and games, and simple modern text editors.

Basically, while it's technically possible, it's not something you'll probably want to do. Yes, Windows apps will run on the Raspberry Pi: But why would you bother?

CAN THE RASPBERRY PI 4 RUN UBUNTU?

It can run Ubuntu with various desktops, with the Raspberry Pi Foundation highlighting Ubuntu Mate and Ubuntu Snappy Core as standouts.

WHAT ARE THE RASPBERRY PI 4'S SPECS?

- System-on-a-chip: Broadcom BCM2711
- CPU: Quad-core 1.5GHz Arm Cortex-A72 based processor
- GPU: VideoCore VI
- Memory: 1/2/4GB LPDDR4 RAM
- Connectivity: 802.11ac Wi-Fi / Bluetooth 5.0, Gigabit Ethernet
- Video and sound: 2 x micro-HDMI ports supporting 4K@60Hz displays via HDMI 2.0, MIPI DSI display port, MIPI CSI camera port, 4 pole stereo output and composite video port
- Ports: 2 x USB 3.0, 2 x USB 2.0
- Power: 5V/3A via USB-C, 5V via GPIO header
- Expandability: 40-pin GPIO header

HOW CAN I GET THE MOST FROM MY RASPBERRY PI 4?

It's worth investing in a case to protect the Pi from damage, especially if you're going to be carrying the Pi with you. Note the Pi 4 doesn't fit earlier Pi cases due a change in its layout.

It's also sensible to shell out for a high-speed micro SD card, as outlined below, if performance is important to you.

While the Pi can run many operating systems, if you're after stability and performance then the official Raspbian operating system is a good choice, having been tuned to get the most from the Pi, and thanks to bundling a fast web browser and a decent selection of office and programming software.

One tip if you didn't install the Raspbian OS using the NOOBS installer, and you're running out of space: you can go into the terminal and type 'sudo raspi-config' and then select the option to 'Expand root partition to fill SD card', which will ensure you're using the available space on the card.

HOW CAN I GET HELP WITH THE RASPBERRY PI 4?

With more than 27 million boards sold since the first Pi launched in 2012, the board now boasts a strong community, which helps other users via the official Raspberry Pi site and forums.

HOW DO I KEEP THE RASPBERRY PI 4 UP TO DATE?

If you're running the Pi's official Raspbian operating system then keeping the Pi up to date is relatively straightforward. Just open the terminal and type sudo apt-get update. Once the update is complete, then type sudo apt-get dist-upgrade.

WHAT IS THE POWER CONSUMPTION OF THE RASPBERRY PI 4?

According to tests, the peak power consumption of the Pi 4 is about 7.6W under load and 3.4W when idle.

WHAT RASPBERRY PI 4 KITS ARE AVAILABLE?

There's no shortage of Raspberry Pi kits available, which add everything from speech recognition, to robotic arms to build-it yourself laptops for kids to virtual assistants to the $35 board. Due to the success of the Pi, if you've got an idea for a project, there's probably a kit out there to suit your needs.

WHAT POWER SUPPLY DO I NEED FOR THE RASPBERRY PI 4?

The best choice is the official Raspberry Pi Foundation USB Type-C power supply, which is rated at 5.1V/3A.

WHICH IS THE FASTEST MICRO SD CARD FOR THE RASPBERRY PI 4?

A particularly fast card in a recent round-up was found to be the 32GB Samsung Evo+, which is relatively affordable at less than 10 dollars.

WHAT SIZE MICRO SD CARD DO I NEED FOR THE RASPBERRY PI 4?

If you're installing the official Raspbian OS you'll need at least an 8GB micro SD card, whereas for the Raspbian Lite you'll need a minimum of 4GB.

CAN I USE WI-FI ON THE RASPBERRY PI 4?

Yes, the board supports 802.11ac Wireless LAN (throughput of around 100 Mbps) and Bluetooth 5.0.

CAN I RUN A NETWORK OF RASPBERRY PI 4S?

Yes, and managing and updating the boards should be made simpler by the ability to boot from a network-attached file system using PXE, allowing admins to share operating system images between machines. PXE support will be added by a future firmware update to the Pi 4.

IS THE RASPBERRY PI 4 64-BIT?

Yes, it's a 64-bit board. However, there are limited benefits to the 64-bit processor, outside of a few more operating systems possibly being able to run on the Pi.

Rather than offering a 64-bit version of the official Raspbian operating system, the Raspberry Pi Foundation has said it wants to focus on optimizing the Pi's official Raspbian OS for 32-bit performance to benefit the millions of older, 32-bit Pi boards that have already been sold.

WHO MAKES THE RASPBERRY PI?

The Raspberry Pi boards are designed by a subsidiary of the Raspberry Pi Foundation, a charitable organization dedicated to advancing computer science education, and manufactured at a Sony factory in South Wales. Since its launch, the Pi has been adopted by many schools, and its availability has also coincided with an almost tripling in the number of people applying to study computer science at Cambridge.

The foundation's founder and board co-creator Eben Upton said he began designing the board as a way to inspire children to learn about computing, after being struck by how few people were applying to study computer science at Cambridge in the mid-2000s.

IS THE RASPBERRY PI JUST A MOTHERBOARD?

Yes, in its cheapest $35 incarnation, although there are a wide range of kits available that bundle together extras like cases, leads and electronics for getting started with hardware hacking -- all for an additional cost, of course. This £70 official Raspberry Pi 4 starter kit bundles much of what you need, including a case, bar the monitor, keyboard and mouse.

HOW DO I KNOW WHICH VERSION OF THE RASPBERRY PI I HAVE?

It's literally written on the top side of the board, for example, 'Raspberry Pi 4 Model B' on a Raspberry Pi 4, typically near the upper edge of the board, just underneath the 40-pin header.

HOW CAN I USE THE RASPBERRY PI 4 TO LEARN PROGRAMMING?

The Pi's official Raspbian OS is loaded with software to teach users about programming, including the drag-and-drop coding tool Scratch, and various utilities for writing and debugging using the Python programming language.

CAN I PROGRAM HARDWARE ON THE RASPBERRY PI?

You can, via the row of 40 GPIO (General Purpose Input Output) pins at the top edge of the board. Hardware such as LEDs, sensors and motors can be hooked to these pins so they can interact with the Pi. Writing simple programs will allow you to send or collect signals using the pins, for example to make an LED flash or to read a measurement from an attached sensor.

CAN THE RASPBERRY PI 4 DO SPEECH RECOGNITION?

Yes, a well-known open-source option is Jasper, which can even be installed on the Pi and used without an internet connection.

Most options for speech recognition rely on a cloud service, hence requiring an internet connection, such as Google Speech or Alexa Voice Service.

An easy way to add speech recognition to the Pi is via Google's Voice AIY (Artificial Intelligence Yourself) kit, which provides all the extra hardware needed to turn the Pi into a Google Voice assistant.

CAN I BUILD A CLUSTER OF RASPBERRY PI 4 BOARDS?

You certainly can, one relatively low-cost options is to combine eight boards together into an OctaPi cluster -- whose combined power is far faster than a single board when calculating prime factors, a key task when cracking encryption.

At the extreme end of the scale is this 750 Pi cluster that has been built at the Los Alamos National Laboratory, and which is due to scale up to 10,000 boards in the future.

CAN I TRAIN A NEURAL NETWORK USING THE RASPBERRY PI 4?

No, it's not powerful enough to train neural networks to do anything useful, you're better off using a more powerful computer with a mid to high-end graphics processing unit (GPU) or a dedicated cloud computing instance, such as an AWS P3 or a Google Cloud Platform Cloud TPU (Tensor Processing Unit) instance.

CAN I RUN A NEURAL NETWORK AND DO MACHINE LEARNING ON THE RASPBERRY PI 4?

Yes you can, although you'll likely want to invest in some additional hardware to be effective. For example, Google's Coral USB stick, which accelerates the rate at which the Pi can carry out vision-related tasks, such as facial and object recognition, using its specialized cores. It can accelerate machine-learning models built using Google's TensorFlow Lite library.

IS THERE A RASPBERRY PI 5?

No, and don't expect one for at least a couple of years, based on the time between previous releases of the Pi.

Raspberry Pi Commands

Sometimes it's hard to keep track of all the Raspberry Pi commands you use, so I created a list of some of the most useful and important ones that will make using Linux on the Raspberry Pi a lot easier.

There are two user "modes" you can work with in Linux. One is a user mode with basic access privileges, and the other is a mode with administrator access privileges (AKA super user, or root). Some tasks can't be performed with basic privileges, so you'll need to enter them with super user privileges to perform them. You'll frequently see the prefix sudo before commands, which means you're telling the computer to run the command with super user privileges.

An alternative to entering sudo before each command is to access the root command prompt, which runs every command with super user privileges. You can access root mode by entering sudo su at the command prompt. After entering sudo su, you'll see the root@raspberrypi:/home/pi# command prompt, and all subsequent commands will have super user privileges.

Most of the commands below have a lot of other useful options that I don't mention. To see a list of all the other available options for a command, enter the command, followed by – –help.

General Commands

- **Apt-get update**: Synchronizes the list of packages on your system to the list in the repositories. Use it before installing new packages to make sure you are installing the latest version.

- **Apt-get upgrade**: Upgrades all of the software packages you have installed.

- **Clear**: Clears previously run commands and text from the terminal screen.

Date: Prints the current date.

- **Find / -name example.txt**: Searches the whole system for the file example.txt and outputs a list of all directories that contain the file.

- **Nano example.txt**: Opens the file example.txt in the Linux text editor Nano.

- **Poweroff**: To shutdown immediately.

- **Raspi-config**: Opens the configuration settings menu.

- **Reboot**: To reboot immediately.

- **Shutdown -h now**: To shutdown immediately.

- **Shutdown -h 01:22**: To shutdown at 1:22 AM.

- **Startx**: Opens the GUI (Graphical User Interface).

File and Directory Commands

- **cat example.txt**: Displays the contents of the file example.txt.

- **cd /abc/xyz**: Changes the current directory to the /abc/xyz directory.

- **cp XXX**: Copies the file or directory XXX and pastes it to a specified location; i.e. cp examplefile.txt /home/pi/office/ copies examplefile.txt in the current directory and pastes it into the /home/pi/ directory. If the file is not in the current directory, add the path of the file's location (i.e. cp /home/pi/documents/examplefile.txt /home/pi/office/ copies the file from the documents directory to the office directory).

- **ls -l**: Lists files in the current directory, along with file size, date modified, and permissions.

mkdir example directory: Creates a new directory named example_directory inside the current directory.

- **Mv XXX**: Moves the file or directory named XXX to a specified location. For example, mv examplefile.txt /home/pi/office/ moves examplefile.txt in the current directory to the /home/pi/office directory. If the file is not in the current directory, add the path of the file's location (i.e. cp /home/pi/documents/examplefile.txt /home/pi/office/ moves the file from the documents directory to the office directory). This command can also be used to rename files (but only within the same directory). For example, mv examplefile.txt newfile.txt renames examplefile.txt to newfile.txt, and keeps it in the same directory.

- **Rm example.txt**: Deletes the file example.txt.

- **Rmdir example_directory**: Deletes the directory example_directory (only if it is empty).

- **Scp user@10.0.0.32:/some/path/file.txt**: Copies a file over SSH. Can be used to download a file from a PC to the Raspberry Pi. user@10.0.0.32 is the username and local IP address of the PC, and /some/path/file.txt is the path and file name of the file on the PC.

- **Touch example.txt**: Creates a new, empty file named example.txt in the current directory.

Networking and Internet Commands

- **fconfig**: To check the status of the wireless connection you are using (to see if wlan0 has acquired an IP address).

- **iwconfig**: To check which network the wireless adapter is using.

- **iwlist wlan0 scan**: Prints a list of the currently available wireless networks.

- **iwlist wlan0 scan | grep ESSID**: Use grep along with the name of a field to list only the fields you need (for example to just list the ESSIDs).

- **nmap**: Scans your network and lists connected devices, port number, protocol, state (open or closed) operating system, MAC addresses, and other information.

- **ping**: Tests connectivity between two devices connected on a network. For example, ping 10.0.0.32 will send a packet to the device at IP 10.0.0.32 and wait for a response. It also works with website addresses.

- **wget http://www.website.com/example.txt:** Downloads the file example.txt from the web and saves it to the current directory.

System Information Commands

- **cat /proc/meminfo**: Shows details about your memory.

- **cat /proc/partitions**: Shows the size and number of partitions on your SD card or hard drive.

- **cat /proc/version**: Shows you which version of the Raspberry Pi you are using.

- **df -h**: Shows information about the available disk space.

- **df /**: Shows how much free disk space is available.

- **dpkg – –get–selections | grep XXX**: Shows all of the installed packages that are related to XXX.

- **dpkg – –get–selections**: Shows all of your installed packages.

- **free**: Shows how much free memory is available.

- **hostname -I**: Shows the IP address of your Raspberry Pi.

- **lsusb**: Lists USB hardware connected to your Raspberry Pi.

- **UP key**: Pressing the UP key will print the last command entered into the command prompt. This is a quick way to repeat previous commands or make corrections to commands.

- **vcgencmd measure_temp**: Shows the temperature of the CPU.

- **vcgencmd get_mem arm && vcgencmd get_mem gpu**: Shows the memory split between the CPU and GPU.

Hopefully this list of commands will make navigating Linux on your Raspberry Pi more efficient and enjoyable.

Navigating the Raspberry Pi's Software

Getting Around

There are two ways to get around the Raspberry Pi's software:

1) Desktop Environment

The desktop environment is known as a GUI (Graphical User Interface). This is what you have been using on your personal computer as you open windows, drag and drop items, create new folders, etc. The desktop environment was designed to mimic an actual office desk with a notepad, calculator, and folders to file written documents in. In this guide, I will point out where you can find stuff but I mainly assume that you know how to get around and use a desktop environment.

2) Linux Shell

The shell is a program known as a CLI (Command-Line Interface) because it takes keyboard commands and passes them to the operating system to carry out. Almost all Linux distributions supply a shell program from the GNU Project called Bash. The name is an acronym for Bourne Again SHell that references the author of the original shell program is was derived from, Steve Bourne. You can do the same things within the shell that you can on a desktop. Except instead of clicking on icons you type commands. Command-line is the way people got around computers decades before there was a GUI and in this guide, it is what you will primarily be using.

Using the Desktop Environment

The desktop in an application called LXDE, which is short for Lightweight X11 Desktop Environment. This application already comes installed on the Raspberry Pi bundled with programs ready for you to use.

The desktop is split up into two main areas: the taskbar and desktop area. You can see the wastebasket icon is in the desktop area. This icon is called a shortcut. You can add and remove shortcuts by right-clicking on an application and choosing *create shortcut.*

The taskbar can hold a number of items called applets. From left to right the applets in the pictured taskbar are:

- Menu
- Application Launch Bar
- Task Bar
- Bluetooth
- WiFi Networks
- Volume Control
- CPU Usage Monitor
- Clock
- Ejector

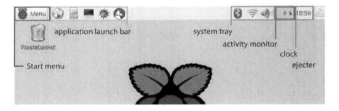

All of these applets in the taskbar can be taken away, added to, and rearranged.

To add or take away applets right-click on the taskbar and choose Add/Remove Panel Items. A window will appear with four tabs running along the top. Click on the tab Panel Applets. Click on Application Launch Bar and then the Preferences button in the right menu.

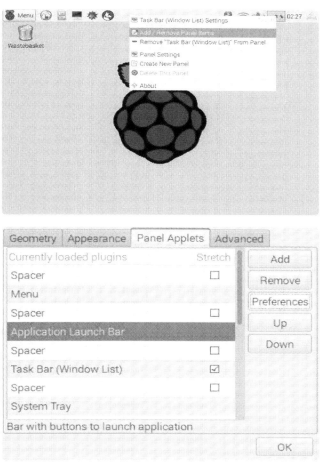

A second window will open that is split into two columns. In the left column, you find the current applications in the application launch bar. The right column holds a list of applications installed on the Pi you can choose to add. As an example, let's remove these two, since we won't be using them in this guide:

- Mathematica
- Wolfram

And add one:

- SonicPi (under "Programming" category)

To remove, click on the application and then the Remove button in the middle. It's that simple! This doesn't delete the program from your Pi, just the shortcut from the taskbar. To add, choose the application from the right column and then click the Add button.

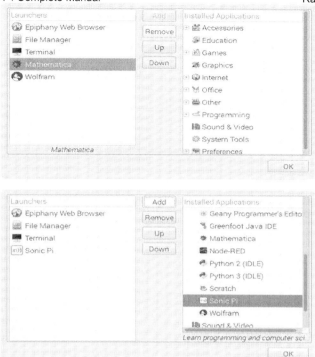

SonicPi's icon is now in the taskbar where the other two apps used to be.

Shutdown + Reboot from GUI

You may have already noticed that the Raspberry Pi 3 (and all other models for that matter) does not have an on/off switch. So, how do you shut off the Raspberry Pi? Simply pulling the power plug while the Raspberry Pi is still running can potentially corrupt the data on the SD card, so don't do that! The best and safest way to switch the Raspberry Pi off is to shut it down through the software. To do this, go to the Menu in the upper left corner and choose Shutdown.

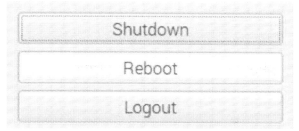

A window pops up with three options

Shutdown

Shutting down your Pi in this way safely stops all processes and shuts down the system. It's extra safe to wait 60 seconds until removing the power supply. Alternatively, you can watch the green ACT LED. It will flash 10 times then become steady notifying it has shutdown.

Reboot

This option safely restarts the Raspberry Pi. This is sometimes necessary after installing the software and configuring the Raspberry Pi.

Logout

The Raspberry Pi can have more than one user in addition to the default Pi user. This option log outs the current user.

Using the File Manager

A large part of a computer's OS is the file system. The File Manager is Raspbian's application for accessing and managing the Raspberry Pi's file system which is comprised of directories (folders) and files (like Windows Explorer or Finder on Mac). Let's open it up and check it out.

Click on the file cabinet icon in the taskbar. You can also find it under Menu > Accessories > File Manager.

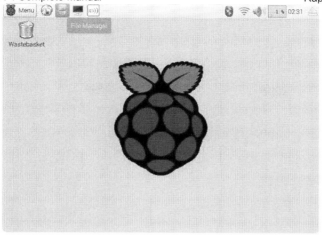

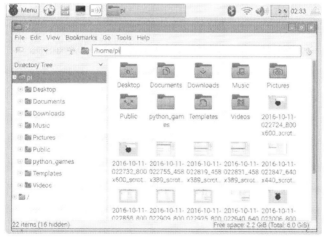

Using the Command-Line Interface

The command-line is also referred to as the terminal or the console. The default terminal application in Raspbian is called LXTerminal. LXTerminal is another program that allows you to interact with the shell. It is technically known as a 'terminal emulator' which means that it emulates the old style video terminals (from before GUIs were developed) in a graphical environment.

To get started we need to open up a terminal window. Press the keys:

Ctrl+Alt+t

Or head to the upper left corner and click on the computer monitor icon with the black screen.

A terminal window will pop up with a short line of characters and a cursor. This is called the command-line prompt.

That line of characters in order from left to right are the **username**, **hostname**, **path**, and **symbol**:

- **username** is the name of the current operating user that is signed into the Pi.
- **hostname** is the name of the Pi
- **path** is where the user is operating from on the computer, also known as the current working directory. The default is the home directory of that user. We are logged in as the user "pi". "~" is the same as the path "/home/username" or "/home/pi" is this case.
- **symbol** indicates what kind of user the current operator is. "$" means normal user "#" means root user.

Using this knowledge, the above line means the user pi is logged into the computer named raspberry pi and is currently in the home directory as a normal user.

The cursor is sitting there waiting for input from you, let's give it something to do!

Take a Screenshot!

For your first task, you will learn how to take a screenshot so you can document your progress throughout the class. To take a screenshot you will use Scrot (SCReenshOT). This is a command line screen capturing application. Scrot comes bundled with Raspbian so there is no need to install it. To take a screenshot of your desktop type:

scrot

The screenshot is automatically saved to your home folder. Go and check it out using the *File Manager*. The screenshot will look like this:

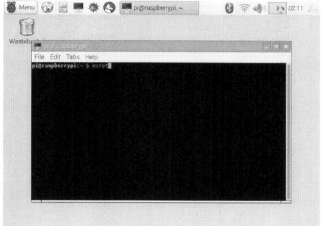

Below are more Scrot commands that will be useful as you document your progress. Try each one and check out the results in the File Manager.

Take a screenshot after a 5-second delay:

scrot -d 5

Countdown a 5-second delay then take a screenshot:

scrot -cd 5

Take a screen shot of the currently active window on the desktop, which in this case is terminal:

scrot -u -cd 5

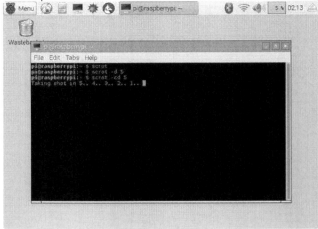

Countdown to screenshot.

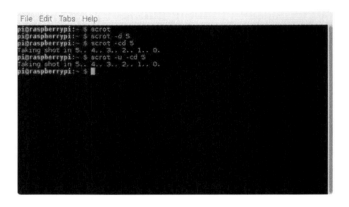

Sudo, Root, and Permissions

The Raspbian operating system allows for more than one user to login to the Raspberry Pi. By default, the Raspberry Pi has two user accounts: pi and root.

Pi is considered a normal user account. Root is a superuser account with additional permissions that allows it to do things a normal user can not. This distinction helps prevent you from accidentally wrecking the operating system and protects the OS from potential viruses. You will mainly stay logged in as a normal user but are able to execute commands as the superuser when needed. This is done by using the command sudo. This command is short for **su**peruser **do**. Putting sudo before another command issues it as the root user giving it root privileges for performing administrative tasks. These tasks include installing software, editing core files, and other powerful tasks.

The Directory Tree

Your Raspberry Pi's file system is arranged in a hierarchical directory structure. This means that the file system is structured as a series of directories branching off from a single directory. As a diagram, the system resembles a tree. To keep in line with a tree analogy in the Raspbian file system the single directory that the directory spawns from is called root.

Path

In the directory tree, each file has a path that points to its location.

Absolute Path

The absolute path is a file's path starting from the root directory. For example, in the File Manager you can see the absolute path of the Documents directory is:

/home/pi/Documents

The first forward slash "/" represents the root directory.

Relative Path

A relative path is the location of a file starting from the current working directory. When you first log into your Raspberry Pi (or start a terminal emulator session) your current working directory is set to your home directory. The relative path of the same Documents directory example used above is:

Documents

Notice how there is no forward slash; this is an indicator that you are using a relative path.

Getting Around and Creating Files

Just like in a desktop environment, you can create and move around files and directories in the command-line. Follow along in a terminal window.

pwd = present working directory. You can always find out where you are in the directory tree with the this command. Try it out:

pwd

mkdir = make a new directory. Put the chosen name of the new directory after mkdir. For example, call this one boof:

mkdir boof

cd = change directory. This command moves you into the directory you point to:

cd boof

The prompt will update with the path of your new location which is now your current working directory:

pi@raspberrypi:~/boof $

While you are in the boof directory make another folder called fotos:

mkdir fotos

Go into the directory called fotos.

cd fotos

ls = list directory contents. To see if there are any files in this directory you can take a look around with the ls command:

ls

When you hit Enter another prompt prints but nothing else. This is because right now the directory you are in is empty. You haven't put any files in it yet (nor boof for matter). Let's create one now by taking a photo with the camera module!

More Useful Command-line Stuff

Command History + Editing

If you find yourself typing similar or the same command repeatedly in the same session you may want to try to copy and paste to save time. Ctrl + C and Ctrl + V won't work in the terminal. Instead, you want to utilize the command history. If you press the up-arrow key you can see and use all your previous commands. To edit a command use the right and left arrows to move the cursor.

Ending a Terminal Session

To end a session and close the terminal window use press Ctrl + D or use:

exit

Or just close the window by clicking your mouse on the X button in the corner.

Snap a Photo!

Raspistill is a lightweight command-line application that comes with Raspbian. It is used to take and manipulate photos with the camera module. So, you know what this means, right? It's time to take a selfie! By default, the camera will show a preview on the screen for 5 seconds before it takes a photo. Position your camera to point towards your face. To take a photo and save it as a jpeg named mePic type:

raspistill -o mePic.jpg

Nice! You just took your first photo with the Raspberry Pi. If there were no errors, you will see a new prompt. If it gave you an error, check for a typo in your command, revisit the configuration to be sure your camera is enabled, and be sure your camera is plugged in properly (requires restart after replugging).

To see if the photo was successfully created, take a look in your cwd (current working directory):

ls

If it is not listed make sure you are at the correct address and try again:

pi@raspberrypi:~/boof/fotos $

If the photo did save correctly, mePic.jpg will be listed. You have now successfully created and moved through files but how do you open them? You can simulate a double-click on a file to open it by using the xdg-open command. Open your picture and check it out:

xdg-open mePic.jpg

You can write over mePic.jpg as many times as you like. You can then email yourself the photos, or load it onto a USB flash drive to copy it from your Raspberry Pi.

Command-line Flags and Getting Help

When you look at these commands you have used so far:

raspistill -o mePic.jpg

scrot -d 5

scrot -u -cd 5

What are -o, -u, -d, and -cd all about? When you see a character with a "-" in front of it this is called a flag. A command-line flag is a common way to specify options for command-line applications and tools such as Scrot and Raspistill. You can look up all the options available for a command-line application and tool with the man command. For example, to take a look at all the options Scrot has to offer type:

man scrot

The man command is short for manual. This brings up the manual pages where you can read a description of the application and all the options available to use.

If you ever want to know more about a command, man is the first thing you should use! You can look up the manual pages for any command using man like so:

man scrot

To exit out of the manual pages press "q".

If a command doesn't have a manual page use -h or --help after a command or application name:

scrot -h

raspistill --help

or info :

info raspistill

I encourage you to use the man and --help commands with every new tool, application, and command you use in LXTerminal. It's an excellent way to learn how to use them, making it a great habit to get in the groove of now.

Programming basics using Python

What is Python?

Python is an interpreted, object-oriented, high-level programming language with dynamic semantics. Its high-level built in data structures, combined with dynamic typing and dynamic binding, make it very attractive for Rapid Application Development, as well as for use as a scripting or glue language to connect existing components together. Python's simple, easy to learn syntax emphasizes readability and therefore reduces the cost of program maintenance. Python supports modules and packages, which encourages program modularity and code reuse. The Python interpreter and the extensive standard library are available in source or binary form without charge for all major platforms, and can be freely distributed.

Often, programmers fall in love with Python because of the increased productivity it provides. Since there is no compilation step, the edit-test-debug cycle is incredibly fast. Debugging Python programs is easy: a bug or bad input will never cause a segmentation fault. Instead, when the interpreter discovers an error, it raises an exception. When the program doesn't catch the exception, the interpreter prints a stack trace. A source level debugger allows inspection of local and global variables, evaluation of arbitrary expressions, setting breakpoints, stepping through the code a line at a time, and so on. The debugger is written in Python itself, testifying to Python's introspective power. On the other hand, often the quickest way to debug a program is to add a few print statements to the source: the fast edit-test-debug cycle makes this simple approach very effective.

Running python programs

You can run python programs in two ways, first by typing commands directly in python shell or run program stored in a file. But most of the time you want to run programs stored in a file.

Lets create a file named hello.py in your documents directory i.e C:\Users\YourUserName\Documents using notepad (or any other text editor of your choice) , remember python files have '.py' extension, then write the following code in the file.

print("Hello World")

In python we use **print** function to display string to the console. It can accept more than one arguments. When two or more arguments are passed, **print** function displays each argument separated by space.

print("Hello", "World")

Expected output

Hello World

Now open terminal and change current working directory to *C:\Users\YourUserName\Documents using cd command.*

To run the program type the following command.

python hello.py

If everything goes well, you will get the following output.

Hello World

Getting Help

Sooner or later while using python you will come across a situation when you want to know more about some method or functions. To help you Python has help() function, here is how to use it.

Syntax:

To find information about class: *help(class_name)*

To find more about method belong to class: *help(class_name.method_name)*

Python Data types

Every value in Python has a datatype. Since everything is an object in Python programming, data types are actually classes and variables are instance (object) of these classes.

There are various data types in Python. Some of the important types are listed below.

Python Numbers

Integers, floating point numbers and complex numbers falls under Python numbers category. They are defined as int, float and complex class in Python.

We can use the type() function to know which class a variable or a value belongs to and the isinstance() function to check if an object belongs to a particular class.

```python
script.py     IPython Shell
1   a = 5
2   print(a, "is of type", type(a))
3
4   a = 2.0
5   print(a, "is of type", type(a))
6
7   a = 1+2j
8   print(a, "is complex number?",
    isinstance(1+2j,complex))
```

Run

Integers can be of any length, it is only limited by the memory available.

A floating point number is accurate up to 15 decimal places. Integer and floating points are separated by decimal points. 1 is integer, 1.0 is floating point number.

Complex numbers are written in the form, x + yj, where x is the real part and y is the imaginary part. Here are some examples.

```
>>> a = 1234567890123456789
>>> a
1234567890123456789
>>> b = 0.1234567890123456789
>>> b
0.12345678901234568
>>> c = 1+2j
>>> c
(1+2j)
```

Notice that the float variable b got truncated.

Python List

List is an ordered sequence of items. It is one of the most used datatype in Python and is very flexible. All the items in a list do not need to be of the same type.

Declaring a list is pretty straight forward. Items separated by commas are enclosed within brackets [ ].

```
>>> a = [1, 2.2, 'python']
```

We can use the slicing operator [ ] to extract an item or a range of items from a list. Index starts form 0 in Python.

```
script.py      IPython Shell
 1    a = [5,10,15,20,25,30,35,40]
 2
 3    # a[2] = 15
 4    print("a[2] = ", a[2])
 5
 6    # a[0:3] = [5, 10, 15]
 7    print("a[0:3] = ", a[0:3])
 8
 9    # a[5:] = [30, 35, 40]
10    print("a[5:] = ", a[5:])
```

Run

Lists are mutable, meaning, value of elements of a list can be altered.

>>> a = [1,2,3]

>>> a[2]=4

>>> a

[1, 2, 4]

Python Tuple

Tuple is an ordered sequence of items same as list.The only difference is that tuples are immutable. Tuples once created cannot be modified.

Tuples are used to write-protect data and are usually faster than list as it cannot change dynamically.

It is defined within parentheses () where items are separated by commas.

>>> t = (5,'program', 1+3j)

We can use the slicing operator [] to extract items but we cannot change its value.

```
script.py      IPython Shell
1    t = (5,'program', 1+3j)
2
3    # t[1] = 'program'
4    print("t[1] = ", t[1])
5
6    # t[0:3] = (5, 'program', (1+3j
     ))
7    print("t[0:3] = ", t[0:3])
8
9    # Generates error
10   # Tuples are immutable
11   t[0] = 10
```

    Run

String is sequence of Unicode characters. We can use single quotes or double quotes to represent strings.

Multi-line strings can be denoted using triple quotes, ''' or """.

>>> s = "This is a string"

>>> s = '''a multiline

Like list and tuple, slicing operator [ ] can be used with string. Strings are immutable.

```
script.py     IPython Shell
1      s = 'Hello world!'
2
3      # s[4] = 'o'
4      print("s[4] = ", s[4])
5
6      # s[6:11] = 'world'
7      print("s[6:11] = ", s[6:11])
8
9      # Generates error
10     # Strings are immutable in
       Python
11     s[5] ='d'
```

Run

Set is an unordered collection of unique items. Set is defined by values separated by comma inside braces { }. Items in a set are not ordered.

```
script.py     IPython Shell
1  a = {5,2,3,1,4}
2
3  # printing set variable
4  print("a = ", a)
5
6  # data type of variable a
7  print(type(a))




Run
```

We can perform set operations like union, intersection on two sets. Set have unique values. They eliminate duplicates.

>>> a = {1,2,2,3,3,3}

>>> a

{1, 2, 3}

Since, set are unordered collection, indexing has no meaning. Hence the slicing operator [] does not work.

>>> a = {1,2,3}

>>> a[1]

```
Traceback  (most recent call last):
    File "<string>", line 301, in runcode
    File "<interactive input>", line 1, in <module>
TypeError: 'set'  object does not support indexing
```

Python Dictionary

Dictionary is an unordered collection of key-value pairs.

It is generally used when we have a huge amount of data. Dictionaries are optimized for retrieving data. We must know the key to retrieve the value.

In Python, dictionaries are defined within braces {} with each item being a pair in the form key:value. Key and value can be of any type.

```
>>> d = {1:'value','key':2}
>>> type(d)
<class 'dict'>
```

We use key to retrieve the respective value. But not the other way around.

```
script.py    IPython Shell
1    d = {1:'value','key':2}
2    print(type(d))
3
4    print("d[1] = ", d[1]);
5
6    print("d['key'] = ", d['key']);
7
8    # Generates error
9    print("d[2] = ", d[2]);




Run
```

What are iterators in Python?

Iterators are everywhere in Python. They are elegantly implemented within for loops, comprehensions, generators etc. but hidden in plain sight.

Iterator in Python is simply an object that can be iterated upon. An object which will return data, one element at a time.

Technically speaking, Python iterator object must implement two special methods, __iter__() and __next__(), collectively called the iterator protocol.

An object is called iterable if we can get an iterator from it. Most of built-in containers in Python like: list, tuple, string etc. are iterables.

The iter() function (which in turn calls the __iter__() method) returns an iterator from them.

Iterating Through an Iterator in Python

We use the next() function to manually iterate through all the items of an iterator. When we reach the end and there is no more data to be returned, it will raise StopIteration. Following is an example.

```
script.py      IPython Shell
1    # define a list
2    my_list = [4, 7, 0, 3]
3
4    # get an iterator using iter()
5    my_iter = iter(my_list)
6
7    ## iterate through it using next
     ()
8
9    #prints 4
10   print(next(my_iter))
11
12   #prints 7
13   print(next(my_iter))
14
15   ## next(obj) is same as obj
     .__next__()
16
17   #prints 0
18   print(my_iter.__next__())
19
20   #prints 3
21   print(my_iter.__next__())
22
23   ## This will raise error, no
```

A more elegant way of automatically iterating is by using the for loop. Using this, we can iterate over any object that can return an iterator, for example list, string, file etc.

>>> *for element in my_list:*

...   *print(element)*

...

4

7

0

3

How for loop actually works?

As we see in the above example, the for loop was able to iterate automatically through the list.

In fact the for loop can iterate over any iterable. Let's take a closer look at how the for loop is actually implemented in Python.

for element in iterable:

    # do something with element

Is actually implemented as.

 # create an iterator object from that iterable

iter_obj = iter(iterable)

 # infinite loop

while True:

    try:

        # get the next item

        element = next(iter_obj)

        # do something with element

   except StopIteration:

     # if StopIteration is raised, break from loop

     break

So internally, the for loop creates an iterator object, iter_obj by calling iter() on the iterable.

Ironically, this for loop is actually an infinite while loop.

Inside the loop, it calls next() to get the next element and executes the body of the for loop with this value. After all the items exhaust, StopIteration is raised which is internally caught and the loop ends. Note that any other kind of exception will pass through.

Building Your Own Iterator in Python

Building an iterator from scratch is easy in Python. We just have to implement the methods __iter__() and __next__().

The __iter__() method returns the iterator object itself. If required, some initialization can be performed.

The __next__() method must return the next item in the sequence. On reaching the end, and in subsequent calls, it must raise StopIteration.

Here, we show an example that will give us next power of 2 in each iteration. Power exponent starts from zero up to a user set number.

```python
script.py    IPython Shell
 2          """Class to implement an iterator
            of powers of two"""
 3
 4
 5 ▾    def __init__(self, max = 0):
 6            self.max = max
 7
 8 ▾    def __iter__(self):
 9            self.n = 0
10            return self
11
12 ▾    def __next__(self):
13 ▾        if self.n <= self.max:
14                result = 2 ** self.n
15                self.n += 1
16                return result
17 ▾        else:
18                raise StopIteration
```

Run

Now we can create an iterator and iterate through it as follows.

>>> a = PowTwo(4)

>>> i = iter(a)

>>> next(i)

1

>>> next(i)

2

```
>>> next(i)
4
>>> next(i)
8
>>> next(i)
16
>>> next(i)
Traceback  (most recent call last):
...
StopIteration
```

We can also use a for loop to iterate over our iterator class.

```
>>> for i in PowTwo(5):
...     print(i)
...
1
2
4
8
16
32
```

Python Infinite Iterators

It is not necessary that the item in an iterator object has to exhaust. There can be infinite iterators (which never ends). We must be careful when handling such iterator.

Here is a simple example to demonstrate infinite iterators.

The built-in function iter() can be called with two arguments where the first argument must be a callable object (function) and second is the sentinel. The iterator calls this function until the returned value is equal to the sentinel.

```
>>> int()
0
>>> inf = iter(int, 1)
>>> next(inf)
0
>>> next(inf)
0
```

We can see that the int() function always returns 0. So passing it as iter(int,1) will return an iterator that calls int() until the returned value equals 1. This never happens and we get an infinite iterator.

We can also built our own infinite iterators. The following iterator will, theoretically, return all the odd numbers.

```python
class InfIter:
    """Infinite iterator to return all
    odd numbers"""

    def __iter__(self):
        self.num = 1
        return self

    def __next__(self):
        num = self.num
        self.num += 2
        return num
```

script.py IPython Shell

Run

A sample run would be as follows.

```
>>> a = iter(InfIter())
>>> next(a)
1
>>> next(a)
3
>>> next(a)
5
```

>>> next(a)

7

And so on...

Be careful to include a terminating condition, when iterating over these type of infinite iterators.

The advantage of using iterators is that they save resources. Like shown above, we could get all the odd numbers without storing the entire number system in memory. We can have infinite items (theoretically) in finite memory.

Iterator also makes our code look cool.

Raspberry pi 4 Projects

Robot antenna

Introduction

In this resource you will build a cardboard robot with a real flashing LED antenna, and use Scratch to create a robot twin that beeps.

What you will make

Here is an example of the robot we made:

What you will need

Hardware:

- A Raspberry Pi 4 and associated peripherals
- 1× LED
- 1× resistor (any resistor above 100 ohms will be fine)
- 4× female-to-female jumper lead
- A mini speaker or headphones

Software

You will need the latest version of Raspbian.

Additional craft materials

- Cardboard toilet roll
- One sheet of A4 paper
- Sharp pencil
- Pens, crayons, and other decorating materials
- Glue or tape
- Small blob of modelling clay (e.g. plasticine or Blu Tack)
- Scissors

What you will learn

- How to connect an LED to a Raspberry Pi.
- How to control an LED with Scratch 3

Make an antenna

Let's get hands-on with electronics! Your first step will be to connect your light-emitting diode (LED) to some jumper wires and a resistor.

First, look at your LED. It has a short leg and a long leg.

- Slot a jumper wire onto the end of the long leg.
- Slot the resistor into the other end of the same jumper wire. It doesn't matter which way round it goes.
- Add another jumper wire to the other end of the resistor.
- Take another jumper wire and slot one end onto the short leg of the LED.

You should end up with something that looks like this:

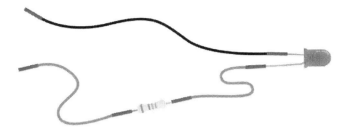

Connect your antenna

Now let's connect the antenna to the Raspberry Pi to make a circuit.

- Make sure your Raspberry Pi is switched off.
- Turn your Raspberry Pi so that it is facing the same way as the one in the diagram below:

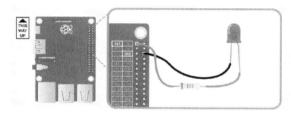

- Look at the pins which are sticking out of the top right of your Raspberry Pi. These pins let the Raspberry Pi communicate with the outside world.
- Take the jumper wire that is connected to the resistor and plug it onto the pin labelled 3V3 on the diagram. This pin provides power to the LED,

so it's rather like connecting the LED to the positive side of a battery.

- Take the jumper wire that is connected to the short leg of the LED and plug it onto the pin labelled GND on the diagram. This pin provides grounding to the LED, like connecting it to the negative side of a battery would do.

- When you have plugged in both wires, you have a circuit.

Power on your Raspberry Pi, and your LED should switch on. If it is not, make sure that you have plugged the jumper wires into the correct pins by checking the diagram above.

Make the antenna flash with code

Now you have an antenna that lights up, let's write a program to tell the LED when to turn on and off.

- Shut your Raspberry Pi down and remove the power cable.

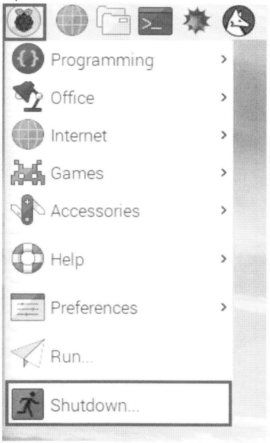

- Move the jumper wire that is connected to the resistor from the 3V3 pin to the pin which is labelled **17** in the diagram below:

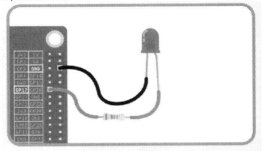

Pin 17 is different to 3V3: you can program it to switch the power on and off.

- Power on your Raspberry Pi and wait for it to boot.
- Open Scratch 3 by clicking on the menu and then Programming, followed by Scratch 3.

- Remove the Scratch cat by right-clicking on it and choosing delete from the menu.

- Click on the button for a new sprite and search for a robot, or, if you prefer, you can draw your own.

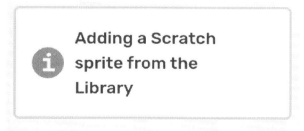

- Click on **Events**. Drag the when space key pressed block into the Scripts area.

- Click on Sound, drag the play sound block into the Scripts area and connect it to the previous block.

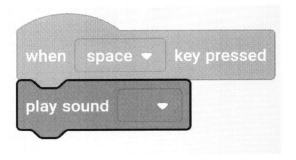

- Add a sound for your robot. We chose the computer beeps from the electronic section.

Adding a sound from the library

Go back to the Scripts tab. Click on the drop-down box in your play sound block and select the sound you just added.

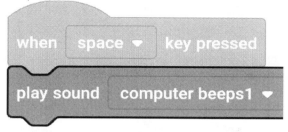

- Test that your program is working so far by pressing the space key. In response, your robot should beep!
- Save your work by clicking File, then Save project, and call it robot.sb3.

Now let's program the LED to flash.

- Next add the Raspberry Pi Simple Electronics extension.

- Select More blocks and then drag this block to the bottom of your script:

- This block allows you to specify a GPIO pin that your LED is wired to.
- Select **17** from the dropdown to specify pin 17, and leave the next drop-down as on. This block will turn your LED on.

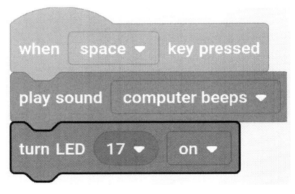

- Add a block to **wait 1 secs** from the control tab.

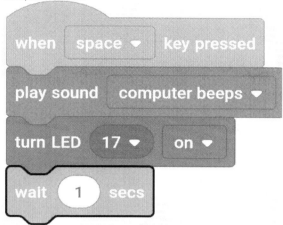

- Now add another LED block, but this time ask it to set it to off.

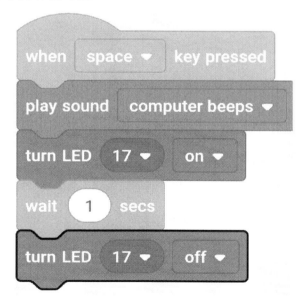

- Test your program by pressing the space key. You should see the LED turn on for a second and then turn off, and your robot should beep.

Make a cardboard robot

Let's make a cardboard robot to display the antenna you've made.

- On a sheet of A4 paper, draw or print your own robot design. It doesn't have to be a person robot — maybe it could be a car or an animal! Just make sure it has an antenna.
- Color in the robot picture and cut it out carefully.
- Wrap the robot around the cardboard tube lengthways.

- Glue or tape the robot in place.
- Stick some modelling clay behind the robot's antenna inside the cardboard tube.

- Push a pencil into the antenna to make a hole through the cardboard tube.

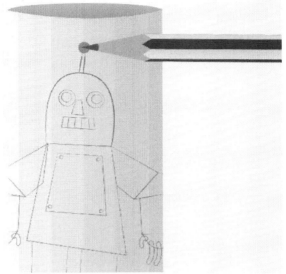

- Remove the modelling clay.
- Put your circuit of jumper wires, LED, and resistor inside your cardboard tube. Push your LED through the hole in the tube to make the robot's antenna.
- Give your robot a name and welcome it to the world!

Challenge: beeps and flashes
- Make the LED antenna stay on for longer.
- Make the LED flash more than once.
- Record your own sound for the robot to make — get creative!

IoT Smart Garage Door Opener using Raspberry Pi

In this age of IoT (Internet of Things) where everything can be controlled remotely using your smartphone, why to carry keys with you. There are lots of technologies to support wireless controlling devices like RFID, Bluetooth, Wi-Fi, LoRa.

Here in this guide, we will build a Smart Garage Door Opener using Raspberry Pi. Here, a Raspberry Pi web server will be created to open and close the garage door using your smartphone.

Components Required

- Raspberry pi board with Raspbian installed in it
- Relay Module
- Connecting Wires

It is assumed that your Raspberry Pi is already flashed with an operating system and is able to connect to the internet.

Here External Monitor using HDMI cable is used as display to connect with Raspberry Pi. If you don't have a monitor, you can use SSH client (Putty) or VNC server to connect to Raspberry pi using Laptop or computer.

Circuit Diagram

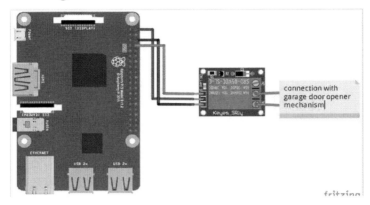

Connect the Garage door opening mechanism to the output of the relay. Here we have just connected an LED with relay for demonstration purpose.

Flask Setup in Raspberry Pi for Controlling Garage Door

Here, we have created a web server using Flask, which provides a way to send the commands from webpage to Raspberry Pi to control the Robot over the network. Flask allows us to run our python scripts through a webpage and we can send & receive data from Raspberry Pi to web browser and vice versa. Flask is a microframework for Python. This tool is Unicode based having built-in development server and debugger, integrated unit testing support, support for secure cookies and its easy to use, these things make it useful for the hobbyist.

Run the following commands to install the flask in your Raspberry Pi:

```
sudo apt-get update
sudo apt-get install python-pip python-flask
```

Now, run the pip command to install Flask and its dependencies:

```
sudo pip install flask
```

Now, we will write a python script for our garage door web server.

Creating the Python Script for Smart Garage Door Opener

This script will interact with our Raspberry Pi GPIOs and sets up the web server. So, this is the core script for our application. Complete Python Script for door opener is given at the end, here we have explained few parts of it.

First, make a folder. All other required folders should be in this folder only. Run below commands to make folder and the create python file named app.py inside this folder.

mkdir garage_door

cd garage_door

nano app.py

This will open the Nano editor where we have to write the script.

Start by including important libraries.

import RPi.GPIO as GPIO

from flask import Flask, render_template, request

app = Flask(__name__, static_url_path='/static')

Now, create a dictionary as pins to store the pin number, name, and pin state. You can use more than one pin according to your need.

pins = {

   14 : {'name' : 'Garage Door', 'state' : GPIO.LOW}

   }

Then, set the pin as output and make it low initially.

For pin in pins:

   GPIO.setup(pin, GPIO.OUT)

   GPIO.output(pin, GPIO.LOW)

Now, make a main function to read pin state and store this state in a variable.

```python
@app.route("/")
def main():
    for pin in pins:
        pins[pin]['state'] = GPIO.input(pin)
..
```

We have to pass this data to our html page so that we can control the input button state.

```python
    return render_template('main.html', **templateData)
```

Now, make a function to handle the requests from the URL with the pin number and action in it.

```python
@app.route("/<changePin>/<action>", methods=['GET', 'POST'])
def action(changePin, action):
```

Convert the pin from the URL into an integer.

```python
    changePin = int(changePin)
```

If the action part of the URL is "open," then do the following.

```python
    if action == "open":
        GPIO.output(changePin, GPIO.HIGH)
    if action == "close":
        GPIO.output(changePin, GPIO.LOW)
```

You can copy the complete script from the end of this tutorial and save it using ctrl+x and then press enter. We have done with the python script. Now, we have to make a HTML page to interact with the python script.

Creating HTML page for Raspberry Pi Webserver

In the same garage_door folder, create another folder named templates and inside this folder make an .html file using below commands.

mkdir templates

cd templates

nano main.html

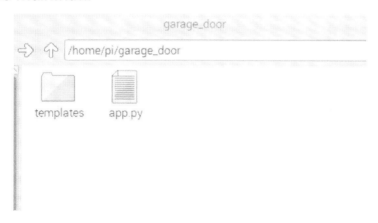

In the nano text editor, write the html code. You can edit the <head> part of the page and style it according to your choice. I have just used the third party css scheme using link tag. The complete HTML code is given below:

```
<!DOCTYPE html>
<head>
   <title>Garage  Door Web server</title>
                     <link              rel="stylesheet"
href="https://www.w3schools.com/w3css/4/w3.css">
                                       <script
src="https://maxcdn.bootstrapcdn.com/bootstrap/3.3.6/j
s/bootstrap.min.js"></script>
</head>
<center>
<body>
   <h1>Garage  Door Web server</h1>
   {% for pin in pins %}
   <h2>{{ pins[pin].name }}
   {% if pins[pin].state == true %}
         is  currently  <strong>Open</strong></h2><div
class="row"><div class="col-md-2">
      <a  href="/{{pin}}/close"  class="w3-button  w3-blue"
role="button">Close</a></div></div>
   {% else %}
```

is currently <strong>Close</strong></h2><div class="row"><div class="col-md-2">

<a href="/{{pin}}/open" class="w3-button w3-black" role="button">Open</a></div></div>

{% endif %}

{% endfor %}

</body>

</center>

</html>

Here the important part is to create a button to open and close the door and assign a state to open and close button. The button will send and fetch the GPIO state from the python script.

You can use the above given HTML code in the editor and save it. Now the web server is ready to launch.

Open the terminal and navigate to garage_door folder and run the below command

sudo python app.py

Open the browser and enter your raspberry pi IP address and hit enter. To find your IP address you can run the below command in terminal.

hostname -I

You will see a page like this.

Make sure the relay module is connected to raspberry pi. Press Open button to switch on the Relay or to open the Garage Door. You can also see the state of the relay. As soon as you turned On the Relay, button text will be changed Close to turn off the relay. Now when you click the button again the relay will be turned off and the button text will be changed to Open again.

To stop the server press ctrl+c .

So just connect this relay to some Door Opener mechanism, which are readily available in market, and start controlling the garage door using Smartphone.

Code:

```
import RPi.GPIO  as GPIO
from flask import Flask, render_template, request
app = Flask(__name__, static_url_path='/static')
GPIO.setmode(GPIO.BCM)
pins = {
   14 : {'name' : 'Garage Door', 'state' : GPIO.LOW}
   }
for  pin in pins:
   GPIO.setup(pin,  GPIO.OUT)
   GPIO.output(pin,  GPIO.LOW)

@app.route("/")
def main():
   for pin in pins:
     pins[pin]['state'] =  GPIO.input(pin)
   templateData = {
     'pins' : pins
```

```python
    }
    return render_template('main.html', **templateData)
@app.route("/<changePin>/<action>", methods=['GET', 'POST'])
def action(changePin, action):
  changePin = int(changePin)
  deviceName = pins[changePin]['name']
  if action == "open":
    GPIO.output(changePin, GPIO.HIGH)
  if action == "close":
    GPIO.output(changePin, GPIO.LOW)
  for pin in pins:
    pins[pin]['state'] = GPIO.input(pin)
  templateData = {
    'pins' : pins
  }
  return render_template('main.html', **templateData)
if __name__ == "__main__":
  app.run(host='0.0.0.0', port=80, debug=True)
GPIO.cleanup()
```

Astronaut Reaction Time Game

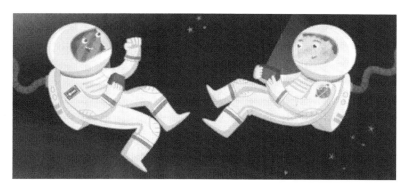

What you will make

In this activity, you will learn about Astronaut reaction times, and distances travelled by the International Space Station in that time, by creating a reaction time game in Scratch.

For the first time ever, a British astronaut from the European Space Agency is going to live and work on the International Space Station. British ESA Astronaut Tim Peake is going to orbit the earth for half a year.

What you will learn

By creating a Scratch reaction game you will learn:

- Why astronauts need to have super-sharp reactions in space, and the average distance travelled by the ISS.

- How to import images into Scratch and use them as backgrounds and sprites.
- How to store data like time and distance in variables.
- Use multiplying operators to calculate distance travelled by the ISS.

What you will need

- A computer with Scratch 1.4

Astronaut Reaction Times Game

Things happen quickly when you're travelling at 16,000 miles per hour (around 7,000 metres per second), and when debris and micrometeoroids are heading towards you at around 22,500 miles per hour. Quick reactions and a steady hand are also needed for tasks requiring fine motor skills, such as controlling robotic arms. Astronauts are trained intensively to speed up their reactions to incidents, and to prepare them for all eventualities.

NASA scientists have conducted experiments to test astronaut reaction times. Astronauts were first tested using a computer system on the ground, then again when they were on board the ISS, and once more when they returned. It was found their reaction times more than doubled in space. Scientists suggest

that stress, as well as the brain having to adapt to microgravity, could be the

cause of this, and that normal performance was found soon after returning to Earth.

Let's create a game in Scratch to test your reaction skills, and those of your friends and family, to see if you could become an astronaut like Tim Peake.

Set the stage with a space theme

If you are using a Raspberry Pi you can open Scratch by clicking on Menu and Programming, followed by Scratch. Alternatively, you can use Scratch 2.0 online for this activity although some of the blocks may be slightly different.

- Create a new file by selecting File and New.
- Delete the Scratch Cat sprite by right-clicking on it and selecting Delete from the menu that is displayed.
- For this project, you need a space-themed background and an Astronaut sprite. To add a

background in Scratch, click on stage in the sprites palette and then click on Backgrounds next to the scripts tab.

- Click on Paint to draw your own background or import to use the same images as this resource.

- Connect your Raspberry Pi to the internet, and download the Space background and British ESA astronaut Tim Peake sprite. Save them somewhere that you will be able to find them on your Raspberry Pi.

- Next, add a new sprite by clicking on the import a new sprite icon on the sprites palette (which looks like the image below), selecting Astronaut-Tim from the choices and clicking OK.

- Save your Scratch project work by clicking on File and Save As. Name your program Astronaut Reaction Game and save it in your home directory or some place that you can find it later.

Create variables to store data

- To create a variable, click on Variables in the blocks palette and then click Make a Variable.

The New Variable window opens and asks you to type a name for your variable.

- Name the first variable time and ensure that For all sprites is checked before clicking OK.

A variable holds a value that can be changed. The time variable you have created is an example of a value that can be changed and used inside different scripts. You will use it to store the reaction times of players.

You'll see some orange blocks are added to your Variable area called time, and a small counter box will appear on the stage.

Begin the reaction game script

- Click on your Sprite to select it in the sprites palette.

- Select the When green flag is clicked control block from the blocks palette and place it onto the scripts area.

- Then click on Looks and connect the say for 2 secs block to the first control block on the scripts area. Amend the text to say Hello! British ESA Astronaut Tim Peake here. Are you ready?.

- Add a wait 1 secs block underneath.

- Connect another say block and change the text to Hit Space!.
- Click on Sensing and connect the reset timer block.

This will set the timer to 0 so that you will get an accurate measurement of how long it takes for someone to hit the space bar.

- Use the control block wait until and place a key space pressed? sensing block inside the white space of the wait until block.

This will pause the program until the player presses the space bar.

- Then connect another say block. Once the space bar has been pressed, you want to display the reaction to the player. To do this, you need to place an operators block called join hello world inside the white space in the say block. Replace the word world with the word seconds.
- You will then need to replace the word Hello with another join hello world operators block, replacing the Hello text with Your reaction time was and the world text with the timer sensing block.

- Finally, select the set time to block from the variables section and add it to your script. Place the timer sensing block inside where it reads 0.

```
when clicked
say Hello British ESA Astronaut Tim Peake here. Are you ready? for 2 secs
wait 1 secs
say Hit Space!
reset timer
wait until key space pressed
say join join Your reaction time was timer seconds
set time to timer
```

Save your game and test it works by clicking on the green flag. When Tim says "Hit Space!", press the space bar. Your time should be displayed like this:

Comparing player's reaction time to the ISS orbit

If you are happy with your reaction game and have tested that it works, then you can move onto adding to the script to compare the player's reaction time to how fast the ISS is travelling, to calculate how far it would travel in that time.

- First you will need to make a new variable called distance in the same way you did earlier.
- Attach a set distance to variable block to your script. Place an operators multiply block 0*0 inside where it reads 0.
- To calculate the distance travelled by the ISS you need to take the player's reaction time, which is stored in the time variable, and multiply it by 7. This is because on average the ISS travels 7 kilometres per second!
- Add the time variable block into the right hand side of the multiplying operator and type 7 in the other side, so that the whole block reads set distance to time * 7.
- Next, add a wait 4 seconds control block.
- Then add a say block. As in the previous step, place a join hello world block inside. Replace

World with kilometres. Insert another join Hello World block to replace Hello. Replace the Hello text in this new Join block with the text In that time the ISS travels around. Then replace World with a round operator block and fill the white space with the distance variable block like this:

Save your game and test that it works by clicking on the green flag.

What next?

- You could make the game more interactive by getting the Tim Peake sprite to ask for the player's name before they start and storing that information in a new name variable. Then you would be able to personalise the say blocks to include the player's name.
- Using some of the other images, could you change the background and sprites to make the game more interesting?
- If you have a Sense HAT, could you use it to trigger the timer instead of pressing the space bar?

Thank you for purchasing our guide, we believe you have been able to master your raspberry Pi 4.

Printed in Great Britain
by Amazon